Meditation in COLORS

Adult Coloring Book

© 2017 M.B. Kos. All Rights Reserved.

Mandalas by M.B. Kos

No part of this book may be reproduced or trasmitted by any form or by any means, electronic or mechanical, including photocopy, recording, or any information storage or retrieval system, without prior written consent from the author.

www.binepublishing.com

The pages of this book are suitable for colored pencils, markers and a variety of other media.
To help prevent bleed through, place a blank sheet between the pages when coloring.

Close your eyes. Relax. Take a deep breath. Inhale through your nose, exhale through your mouth. Repeat the breathing exercise. In your mind, imagine the colors you will use. Imagine the pattern of colors. Meditate on your decision. Color the mandala and implement your meditation.